PILLOW
TALK

A 365 Day Journal for Couples to Enhance Intimacy through Communication

Sada' S. Torrey

Printed in the United States of America

First Printing, 2015

ISBN 978-1-941749-22-7

4-P Publishing
Chattanooga, TN 37411

Connect with Sada' Strickland Torrey on Facebook for more updates.

If you are interested in writing a book, connect with SWAT Book Writing Camp at www.swatbookcamp.com

DEDICATION

For My Groom & My J Girls,
I Love You All Dearly

ACKNOWLEDGMENTS

My Savior, I acknowledge You for everything that You are to me. You have saved me, changed me, loved me, and "kept" me like none other. I thank You for all You have done and all that You have shown me I can become. I am eternally grateful to You for loving me even before I learned to love myself. Thank You!

To my husband Jamal, who pushed me to start this journey, even though I was nowhere near "ready." Even when I had no idea of what to write, even when I didn't know if I could do it, or how I was going to do it. When times got hard and my ideas wouldn't work, and I had to start over again and again, you pushed me on, told me to keep going. When I got behind you kept pushing me. Now that this work is done, I appreciate you for planting the seeds of perseverance within me. Without your pushes, over the edge, this book wouldn't be possible. I would still be sitting on the cliff wondering if I could do it or wondering when will I ever? By pushing me to complete this you have helped hundreds and hopefully thousands of marriages without even writing one page! Your "Gavin fund" is growing! I love you!

My J Girls, J'Asia, Ja'Niyah, and Jay'Leigh, you all do not know how much you inspire me to reach my highest potential. As God entrusted each of you to me, each one of your births pushed me to become a greater woman and a greater mom and it is my wish that my life and my example does the same for you. Thank you for your patience during this process and allowing me to pursue this bucket list dream.

To my mom, Marlene and the rest of my family, I could say so much about you all, but that's a whole book series within itself. So for now, I will say thank you for Sunday dinners, laughter, fun memories, the jokes and being super crazy! I love you all!

It takes a village to write a book, but it's even more amazing when that village is wrapped up in one person. I send love and light to you, Laura, for being my coach, mentor, accountability partner, peer reviewer, publisher, teacher, inspiration, ministry partner and the list goes on. Thank you for walking in your purpose! You are such an excellent teacher and I genuinely appreciate you. Without your continuous accountability, I don't know how long it would have taken to "show up" to write, publish, submit, and every other task we had to complete. You were whooping our butts every two weeks to sit down and get it done and now look at what we've accomplished together! Who would have thought?

To Dr. Banks and Lady Sylvia, my pastor and beautiful first lady. You two are priceless! I have never met a couple so real, so loving, and so pure. My life has been forever changed as a result of your teachings, your love, your example, your leadership, your time and everything else you give. Thank you for your friendship! It means the world to me.

My Empowerment Family, aka, the "foot in the back ministry!" I just smile and laugh thinking of all the things you all push me to do. In the short time we've known each other I have started a summer camp and written a book in less than a year and you all have been supporting me, pushing me, and accepted me since day one. You are so precious to me. I am so blessed to have this circle to support me in fulfilling my purpose, reaching my highest potential, and pursuing my passions. Thank you for letting me be me and loving me as I am.

COMMUNICATE, GROW, CONNECT...

Welcome to the Pillow Talk Journaling Experience.

Many couples dream of having a harmonious marriage that encompasses friendship, love, and oneness. We want a marriage where we feel connected to our mate, support one another's needs and we engage on the deepest level of affection.

One of the biggest barriers to the dream of what we think is a perfect marriage is communication. Without communication, it's impossible to have friendship. It becomes an impossible mission to become "one" if we can't communicate, in which direction we will move, to become one. How can we be connected, support one another and find affections, if we don't converse about a vision of what that means to us?

Pillow Talk was created as a tool to help each and every marriage discover who you are as a couple now and to gain awareness of where you would like to go. You are about to discover habits, dreams, ideas and beliefs and so much more, simply by answering questions and communicating.

It is my prayer that you take this journal on with a level of maturity. There will be entertaining conversations that cause you to reminisce about the fun times, as well as dream about the future together. You will be able to compliment your mate and get constant reminders to thank them for all the good they bring to your life. Nonetheless, there will also be challenging discussions that will cause us to be open and honest with ourselves and our spouses. I love this quote by Wayde Goodall, he says, "Married couples must be willing to reveal their thoughts by honest communication. Mature love says, 'This is where I am hurting." Or, 'This is what I do not like." 'This is what I need. What do you need?" "What is hurting you?" We need to stop hiding our feelings and opinions and be honest with each other."

It was also my purpose to make this journal into a learning tool for couples. I considered topics we should know or learn about in marriage and put them in the form of questions to create a self-awareness learning experience. Some couples have never set goals as a couple, realized you should have consistent date nights, found your Love Languages as revealed by Dr. Gary Chapman or learned that a man needs respect more than "love" and a woman needs "unconditional love," more than anything, in order to feel alive (Love & Respect by Dr. Emerson Eggrich). However, as you read and find terms you may have not encountered, that a couple should be engaging in, I urge you to take a deeper look into some of the marital resources and topics. It will only help to improve the quality of your marriage.

Before you start, here are a few helpful tips on how to benefit most from your Pillow Talk journal:

- Use Pillow Talk together as a couple, is a great way to begin growing together in your marriage.
- You may use this book as an individual. If you are looking for answers about your marriage, this book may be able to help you. Journaling is a wonderful way to gain clarity.
- You can buy two separate books and write directly in the book or buy two journals. I found this worked best for my husband and I when we were both writing our thoughts at the same time and then shared our feelings afterward. It gave each of us a chance to express our true, honest feelings without influence from the other person's answers.

Most of all, I pray that you enjoy your "Pillow Talk" Discoveries.

·JANUARY· 1

Spend a few moments to write a letter to your love. Express your love, your dreams, your hopes and gratitude for the upcoming year.

_____
_____
_____
_____
_____
_____
_____
_____
_____
_____
_____
_____

What are our goals for the upcoming year in the following areas: Personal Development, Finances, Career, Marriage, Family, Fun and Community?

_____
_____
_____
_____
_____
_____
_____
_____
_____
_____

·JANUARY· 2

With focus on the goals you wrote yesterday,
connect 3 small action steps to each goal
to get you started.

·JANUARY·

3

_____

_____

_____

_____

_____

_____

_____

_____

_____

_____

_____

_____

_____

Choose just one word this year that we could
focus on to take our marriage to another level.

_____

_____

_____

_____

_____

_____

_____

_____

_____

_____

_____

_____

·JANUARY·

4

·JANUARY· 5

What is our vision for our marriage?
Where do we want our marriage to go?

_____
_____
_____
_____
_____
_____
_____
_____
_____
_____
_____
_____
_____
_____

What we put up with, we end up with.
What do we tolerate in our marriage that
does not serve us in a positive way?

_____
_____
_____
_____
_____
_____
_____
_____
_____
_____
_____
_____
_____

·JANUARY· 6

What actions can we take to work through
conflict in a way that makes us stronger?

·JANUARY·
7

_____
_____
_____
_____
_____
_____
_____
_____
_____
_____
_____
_____

What are 10 things I am
grateful for about my spouse?

_____
_____
_____
_____
_____
_____
_____
_____
_____
_____
_____

·JANUARY·
8

How did we act when we were newlyweds?
Do we still behave like newlyweds?

·JANUARY·
9

_____

_____

_____

_____

_____

_____

_____

_____

_____

_____

_____

_____

_____

When was the last time I pursued
my spouse and made them feel wanted?

_____

_____

_____

_____

_____

_____

_____

_____

_____

_____

_____

_____

·JANUARY·
10

·JANUARY· 11

Bride: Do I feel like I am being properly cared for? Do I feel like my groom provides and protects me?

Groom: Do I feel respected by my bride? Does she help make sure I feel successful?

_____
_____
_____
_____
_____
_____
_____
_____
_____
_____
_____

What expectations do I have for my mate? How do I treat my mate when they fail to meet my expectations?

_____
_____
_____
_____
_____
_____
_____
_____
_____
_____
_____

·JANUARY· 12

·JANUARY· 13

What are some of my favorite ways
to show love to my spouse?

_____
_____
_____
_____
_____
_____
_____
_____
_____
_____
_____
_____
_____
_____

What are some ways I can improve in
loving or respecting my spouse?

_____
_____
_____
_____
_____
_____
_____
_____
_____
_____
_____
_____
_____

·JANUARY· 14

In my opinion, here is what I think it
takes to make a marriage succeed?

·JANUARY·
15

_____
_____
_____
_____
_____
_____
_____
_____
_____
_____
_____
_____
_____

What are some of my favorite
memories from our relationship?

_____
_____
_____
_____
_____
_____
_____
_____
_____
_____
_____
_____
_____

·JANUARY·
16

If I became completely dedicated to one habit
that would change my marriage for the better,
I should focus on?

·JANUARY·
17

_____
_____
_____
_____
_____
_____
_____
_____
_____
_____
_____
_____

Write your vows to one another or write
new vows to renew your commitment.

·JANUARY·
18

_____
_____
_____
_____
_____
_____
_____
_____
_____
_____
_____
_____

Write down plans, hopes and wishes
for your next anniversary.

·JANUARY·
19

_____
_____
_____
_____
_____
_____
_____
_____
_____
_____
_____
_____

When times are hard in marriage,
what is something you want your spouse
to know or remember to help each other make it
through the rough times?

·JANUARY·
20

_____
_____
_____
_____
_____
_____
_____
_____
_____
_____
_____

Are there any stressful situations that my spouse is dealing with and how can I help bear their burden?

·JANUARY·
21

_____
_____
_____
_____
_____
_____
_____
_____
_____
_____
_____
_____
_____

What have we learned about marriage
since we've gained marital experience?

_____
_____
_____
_____
_____
_____
_____
_____
_____
_____
_____
_____

·JANUARY·
22

·JANUARY·
23

I would love for my mate to recognize
and appreciate me more for...

_____
_____
_____
_____
_____
_____
_____
_____
_____
_____
_____
_____
_____

Long-lasting love doesn't happen by accident.
We must be intentional and deliberate about it.
What is one thing we can do more of and one
thing we must do less of to create a marriage we are
proud to have?

_____
_____
_____
_____
_____
_____
_____
_____
_____
_____
_____
_____

·JANUARY·
24

·JANUARY· 25

What dreams would we love to
see come true for us this year?

_____
_____
_____
_____
_____
_____
_____
_____
_____
_____
_____
_____
_____
_____
_____

In what ways would I like to
receive help from my spouse?

_____
_____
_____
_____
_____
_____
_____
_____
_____
_____
_____
_____
_____

·JANUARY· 26

Do I feel supported by my spouse
and if so, in what ways?

·JANUARY·
27

_____
_____
_____
_____
_____
_____
_____
_____
_____
_____
_____
_____
_____
_____
_____

What is going really well in my marriage, right now?
What responsibility did we take to make sure we
could get those great results?

_____
_____
_____
_____
_____
_____
_____
_____
_____
_____
_____
_____
_____
_____

·JANUARY·
28

·JANUARY· 29

What goal do we need to get
focused on together?

_____
_____
_____
_____
_____
_____
_____
_____
_____
_____
_____
_____
_____

Our life is amazing together because...

_____
_____
_____
_____
_____
_____
_____
_____
_____
_____
_____

·JANUARY· 30

·JANUARY·
31

Do I feel there is a level of intimacy and passion in our marriage? Do I feel a connection to my mate?

_____

_____

_____

_____

_____

_____

_____

_____

_____

_____

_____

_____

_____

_____

_____

_____

_____

_____

_____

_____

_____

_____

_____

_____

_____

_____

FEBRUARY
1

What does unconditional love look like to you?

_____
_____
_____
_____
_____
_____
_____
_____
_____
_____
_____
_____
_____
_____
_____

What words would you love to hear from
your mate that would make your day?

_____
_____
_____
_____
_____
_____
_____
_____
_____
_____
_____
_____

FEBRUARY
2

What is your idea of a perfect date?

FEBRUARY
3

_____
_____
_____
_____
_____
_____
_____
_____
_____
_____
_____
_____
_____
_____

What is your favorite physical asset of your spouse?

_____
_____
_____
_____
_____
_____
_____
_____
_____
_____
_____
_____

FEBRUARY
4

FEBRUARY
5

What is a marriage book or advice that
has honestly helped our marriage?

_____
_____
_____
_____
_____
_____
_____
_____
_____
_____
_____
_____
_____
_____

Are we in a healthy and happy marriage?
If yes, what makes our marriage healthy?
If not, what needs to improve to
reach a level that is healthy?

_____
_____
_____
_____
_____
_____
_____
_____
_____
_____
_____
_____

FEBRUARY
6

What are some ways my spouse has
helped me to become a better person?

FEBRUARY

7

_____

_____

_____

_____

_____

_____

_____

_____

_____

_____

_____

_____

_____

Make a list of 12 dates you want to have this year.

_____

_____

_____

_____

_____

_____

_____

_____

_____

_____

_____

_____

_____

FEBRUARY

8

FEBRUARY

9

If I always saw my mate as the king or queen they truly are, how would I treat them differently, than what I do now?

_____
_____
_____
_____
_____
_____
_____
_____
_____
_____
_____
_____
_____
_____

What are we going to plan for Valentine's day?

_____
_____
_____
_____
_____
_____
_____
_____
_____
_____
_____
_____
_____

FEBRUARY

10

FEBRUARY
11

How can I support my spouse?
Where do they need my support the most?

_____
_____
_____
_____
_____
_____
_____
_____
_____
_____
_____
_____
_____
_____
_____

What makes me want to stay in our marriage?

_____
_____
_____
_____
_____
_____
_____
_____
_____
_____
_____

FEBRUARY
12

What are some of your spouse's best qualities?

FEBRUARY
13

_____
_____
_____
_____
_____
_____
_____
_____
_____
_____
_____
_____
_____
_____

What is my favorite love quote?

_____
_____
_____
_____
_____
_____
_____
_____
_____
_____
_____
_____
_____
_____

FEBRUARY
14

FEBRUARY
15

What did you enjoy most about Valentine's Day?

_____
_____
_____
_____
_____
_____
_____
_____
_____
_____
_____
_____
_____

Do we both realize we are on the same team and carry ourselves in such a manner?

_____
_____
_____
_____
_____
_____
_____
_____
_____
_____
_____
_____

FEBRUARY
16

FEBRUARY 17

We are going on _____ years?
That makes me think, feel, or notice what
about our commitment towards one another?

_____
_____
_____
_____
_____
_____
_____
_____
_____
_____
_____
_____
_____
_____
_____

What is stealing my focus from our marriage?

_____
_____
_____
_____
_____
_____
_____
_____
_____
_____
_____

FEBRUARY 18

FEBRUARY
19

My first impression of my mate was...

_____
_____
_____
_____
_____
_____
_____
_____
_____
_____
_____
_____
_____
_____

What is a funny memory
that I have about our marriage?

_____
_____
_____
_____
_____
_____
_____
_____
_____
_____
_____
_____

FEBRUARY
20

FEBRUARY
21

What is my spouse's dream and
how will I help them achieve it?

_____
_____
_____
_____
_____
_____
_____
_____
_____
_____
_____
_____
_____
_____
_____

I need to thank my spouse for...

_____
_____
_____
_____
_____
_____
_____
_____
_____
_____
_____
_____

FEBRUARY
22

FEBRUARY
23

Who are 3 couples we can have as a support team who would encourage us and we could seek guidance and wisdom?

_____
_____
_____
_____
_____
_____
_____
_____
_____
_____
_____
_____
_____
_____
_____
_____

What area of marriage, do I need to improve, to help my marriage succeed?

_____
_____
_____
_____
_____
_____
_____
_____
_____
_____
_____
_____
_____

FEBRUARY
24

FEBRUARY
25

What have I done today to improve my marriage?

_____
_____
_____
_____
_____
_____
_____
_____
_____
_____
_____
_____
_____
_____

What fears do I have about life and marriage?

_____
_____
_____
_____
_____
_____
_____
_____
_____
_____
_____
_____
_____

FEBRUARY
26

FEBRUARY

27

I am proud of my mate for...

_____
_____
_____
_____
_____
_____
_____
_____
_____
_____
_____
_____
_____
_____
_____

What did I look forward to the most
about becoming one with my spouse?

_____
_____
_____
_____
_____
_____
_____
_____
_____
_____
_____
_____
_____
_____

FEBRUARY

28

FEBRUARY

29

What makes us unique as a couple?

_____
_____
_____
_____
_____
_____
_____
_____
_____
_____
_____
_____

_____
_____
_____
_____
_____
_____
_____
_____
_____
_____
_____
_____
_____
_____
_____

I need to forgive my mate for...

_____

_____

_____

_____

_____

_____

_____

_____

_____

_____

_____

_____

march 1

Have we truly committed to overcome all obstacles
and to always find solutions for troubles that
may arise against our marriage?

_____

_____

_____

_____

_____

_____

_____

_____

_____

_____

_____

march 2

Do I feel like my marriage is growing
or stuck in time; and why?

march 3

_____
_____
_____
_____
_____
_____
_____
_____
_____
_____
_____
_____
_____
_____

Write a prayer for your marriage.

_____
_____
_____
_____
_____
_____
_____
_____
_____
_____
_____
_____

march 4

How do I rate our communication and why? What skills do we need to learn to make our communication go to the next level?

march 5

_____
_____
_____
_____
_____
_____
_____
_____
_____
_____
_____
_____
_____
_____

What is a 7-day goal we can work on to promote oneness and practice teamwork?

_____
_____
_____
_____
_____
_____
_____
_____
_____
_____

march 6

march 7

What are 5 things my spouse
could do to become a better spouse?

_____
_____
_____
_____
_____
_____
_____
_____
_____
_____
_____
_____
_____
_____
_____

It's important to strive to stay "one."
How can we reconnect if we find ourselves
losing our connection?

_____
_____
_____
_____
_____
_____
_____
_____
_____
_____
_____
_____

march 8

Write down 10 important dates we have created together. (Ex: First Dates, First kiss, engagement, wedding, births, accomplishments, vacation)

march 9

_____
_____
_____
_____
_____
_____
_____
_____
_____
_____
_____
_____
_____
_____
_____
_____

What is the next goal my spouse wants to reach and how can I offer my support to them?

_____
_____
_____
_____
_____
_____
_____
_____
_____
_____
_____
_____

march 10

If we could take a class to learn something new together, what class would I want to take?

march 11

_____
_____
_____
_____
_____
_____
_____
_____
_____
_____
_____
_____
_____
_____

What is my number one need from my spouse?

_____
_____
_____
_____
_____
_____
_____
_____
_____
_____
_____
_____

march 12

march 13

_____
_____
_____
_____
_____
_____
_____
_____
_____
_____
_____
_____
_____

The strongest degree about our marriage is…

_____
_____
_____
_____
_____
_____
_____
_____
_____
_____
_____
_____

march 14

On a scale of 1-10, how do you rate
your spouse's effort in the marriage?

march 15

_____
_____
_____
_____
_____
_____
_____
_____
_____
_____
_____
_____
_____
_____
_____

This year we will...

_____
_____
_____
_____
_____
_____
_____
_____
_____
_____
_____
_____
_____
_____

march 16

What has surprised you most about your marriage?

_____
_____
_____
_____
_____
_____
_____
_____
_____
_____
_____
_____
_____
_____

march 17

I need to thank my spouse for...

_____
_____
_____
_____
_____
_____
_____
_____
_____
_____
_____
_____

march 18

The #1 thing I love about my spouse is...

_____

_____

_____

_____

_____

_____

_____

_____

_____

_____

_____

_____

_____

_____

march 19

Our latest accomplishment as a team was...

_____

_____

_____

_____

_____

_____

_____

_____

_____

_____

_____

_____

_____

march 20

What do we want our next
biggest accomplishment to be?

_____
_____
_____
_____
_____
_____
_____
_____
_____
_____
_____
_____

march 21

A fun date night would be...

_____
_____
_____
_____
_____
_____
_____
_____
_____
_____
_____

march 22

My spouse inspires me to...

_____

march 23

_____
_____
_____
_____
_____
_____
_____
_____
_____
_____
_____

If I could let my mate know one thing, it would be...

_____
_____
_____
_____
_____
_____
_____
_____
_____
_____

march 24

Who has the biggest influence on our marriage?

_____
_____
_____
_____
_____
_____
_____
_____
_____
_____
_____
_____
_____
_____
_____

march 25

What is my purpose of our lives?
What is the purpose of our marriage?

_____
_____
_____
_____
_____
_____
_____
_____
_____
_____
_____
_____

march 26

What is the biggest obstacle
we have overcome together?

march 27

_____
_____
_____
_____
_____
_____
_____
_____
_____
_____
_____
_____
_____
_____

What is it about my spouse that makes me smile?

march 28

_____
_____
_____
_____
_____
_____
_____
_____
_____
_____
_____
_____
_____

What steps will we take to
affair-proof our marriage?

march 29

_____
_____
_____
_____
_____
_____
_____
_____
_____
_____
_____
_____
_____

What is one thing you hope your spouse never
changes about themselves or their personality?

_____
_____
_____
_____
_____
_____
_____
_____
_____
_____
_____

march 30

march 31

How could we change up our
morning and/or evening routine and
do something different together?

APRIL
1

_____
_____
_____
_____
_____
_____
_____
_____
_____
_____
_____

What do we want our
marriage to demonstrate to others?

APRIL
2

_____
_____
_____
_____
_____
_____
_____
_____
_____
_____
_____

I would love for our next vacation to be...

_____

————— APRIL —————
3

_____

What areas are we in agreement?
Where are we divided?

————— APRIL —————
4

_____

Are there things attacking our marriage that we need to be aware of and make a plan to get rid of the problems? If so, what are they and what are our solutions?

APRIL
5

_____

_____

_____

_____

_____

_____

_____

_____

_____

_____

_____

_____

_____

How do I feel about expressing myself and sharing my feelings with my spouse?

_____

_____

_____

_____

_____

_____

_____

_____

_____

_____

_____

APRIL
6

I am glad we are doing better with...

——— APRIL ———

7

_____
_____
_____
_____
_____
_____
_____
_____
_____
_____
_____
_____
_____

My spouse is amazing because...

_____
_____
_____
_____
_____
_____
_____
_____
_____
_____
_____
_____

——— APRIL ———

8

Would we want our children to
emulate a marriage like ours?

—— APRIL ——
9

_____
_____
_____
_____
_____
_____
_____
_____
_____
_____
_____
_____

Do we seek out marriage education?
Should we start?

—— APRIL ——
10

_____
_____
_____
_____
_____
_____
_____
_____
_____
_____
_____

Making our marriage last forever is important.
What can we do to ensure that we will have a
GREAT MARRIAGE?

APRIL
11

_____
_____
_____
_____
_____
_____
_____
_____
_____
_____
_____
_____
_____
_____

God has really blessed us...

_____
_____
_____
_____
_____
_____
_____
_____
_____
_____
_____
_____

APRIL
12

Have I accepted that my mate and I
are not perfect and will make many mistakes?

APRIL
13

_____

_____

_____

_____

_____

_____

_____

_____

_____

_____

_____

_____

What is going on in my spouses' life right now?
Am I being supportive or neglectful?

_____

_____

_____

_____

_____

_____

_____

_____

_____

_____

_____

_____

APRIL
14

For many couples, falling in love and saying "I DO" was the easy part. Living happily ever after is the part that takes a whole lot of work.
Do you agree or disagree?

APRIL
15

_____
_____
_____
_____
_____
_____
_____
_____
_____
_____
_____
_____

Could I say my spouse is my best friend?

_____
_____
_____
_____
_____
_____
_____
_____
_____
_____
_____
_____
_____

APRIL
16

APRIL
17

_____

_____

_____

_____

_____

_____

_____

_____

_____

_____

_____

_____

Groom: How could I become a better leader?
Bride: How can I support my groom in his role as
leader of our home?

_____

_____

_____

_____

_____

_____

_____

_____

_____

_____

_____

APRIL
18

APRIL
19

_____

_____

_____

_____

_____

_____

_____

_____

_____

_____

_____

Has my spouse and I adopted principles we will live
by to create a successful marriage?
List some below.

_____

_____

_____

_____

_____

_____

_____

_____

_____

_____

_____

APRIL
20

How do we handle disagreements?
What do we need to do different or continue doing
to make sure we win disagreements as a team?

—— APRIL ——
21

_____
_____
_____
_____
_____
_____
_____
_____
_____
_____
_____
_____

In what ways am I seeking attention
and/or appreciation from my spouse?

_____
_____
_____
_____
_____
_____
_____
_____
_____
_____
_____

—— APRIL ——
22

What is something we need to pray for?

APRIL
23

_____
_____
_____
_____
_____
_____
_____
_____
_____
_____
_____
_____
_____

Every love story is beautiful,
but ours is my favorite, why?

_____
_____
_____
_____
_____
_____
_____
_____
_____
_____
_____

APRIL
24

I notice our marriage becomes
disconnected and difficult to deal with when...

APRIL
25

_____

_____

_____

_____

_____

_____

_____

_____

_____

_____

_____

_____

Being open and transparent with myself,
what problems, big or small, am I causing my
marriage that I need to take responsibility for?

_____

_____

_____

_____

_____

_____

_____

_____

_____

_____

_____

APRIL
26

APRIL 27

What did I love about my
spouse when we first became friends?

_____
_____
_____
_____
_____
_____
_____
_____
_____
_____
_____
_____
_____
_____
_____
_____

Can I be totally open with
my spouse about everything?

_____
_____
_____
_____
_____
_____
_____
_____
_____
_____
_____
_____

APRIL 28

What boundaries have we set up in our marriage to keep opposite sex friendships in their proper place?

APRIL 29

_____
_____
_____
_____
_____
_____
_____
_____
_____
_____
_____
_____
_____
_____

Are we enjoying life as a married couple?

_____
_____
_____
_____
_____
_____
_____
_____
_____
_____
_____

APRIL 30

MAY 1

I would like my spouse to encourage me in what areas and what are practical ways I would like to be shown that encouragement?

_____
_____
_____
_____
_____
_____
_____
_____
_____
_____
_____
_____

I need my spouse to...

_____
_____
_____
_____
_____
_____
_____
_____
_____
_____
_____

MAY 2

MAY 3

Our marriage could be
increasingly better if we learned how to...

_____
_____
_____
_____
_____
_____
_____
_____
_____
_____
_____
_____
_____
_____

Does my character and lifestyle
equip me with the ability to have a marriage
that honors God and my spouse?

_____
_____
_____
_____
_____
_____
_____
_____
_____
_____
_____
_____
_____

MAY 4

MAY 5

Make a list of 10 ways I
can serve my spouse this month?

_____

_____

_____

_____

_____

_____

_____

_____

_____

_____

_____

_____

_____

_____

_____

_____

What kind of mark or legacy
do I want to make on my family?

_____

_____

_____

_____

_____

_____

_____

_____

_____

_____

_____

_____

_____

MAY 6

MAY 7

I really appreciate my spouse for...

_____

_____

_____

_____

_____

_____

_____

_____

_____

_____

_____

_____

Do I encourage honesty by allowing my spouse to openly discuss anything or do I make it hard for us to talk freely about anything?

_____

_____

_____

_____

_____

_____

_____

_____

_____

_____

_____

MAY 8

MAY 9

What has too much of my time and attention that may have me neglecting my marriage? Have I considered how this could make my spouse feel?

_____
_____
_____
_____
_____
_____
_____
_____
_____
_____
_____
_____
_____
_____
_____
_____

The best date we've had so far is...

_____
_____
_____
_____
_____
_____
_____
_____
_____
_____
_____
_____
_____

MAY 10

MAY 11

Think about "our song".
Write a couple of your favorite lines from the song
and why you feel it relates to your marriage.

_____
_____
_____
_____
_____
_____
_____
_____
_____
_____
_____
_____
_____
_____

You married because your spouse did a great
job at meeting some of your emotional needs.
Are those needs still being met by your spouse?

_____
_____
_____
_____
_____
_____
_____
_____
_____
_____
_____
_____
_____

MAY 12

MAY 13

Am I still interested in meeting my mate's needs or have I neglected them?

_____
_____
_____
_____
_____
_____
_____
_____
_____
_____
_____
_____

Not everything in marriage comes natural and sometimes requires effort and learning new skills. How does having to put in effort, to create a healthy marriage, make you feel?

_____
_____
_____
_____
_____
_____
_____
_____
_____
_____
_____

MAY 14

MAY 15

Our marriage desire should be to please God.
What direction does God want us to
move toward next in our marriage?

_____
_____
_____
_____
_____
_____
_____
_____
_____
_____
_____
_____
_____
_____
_____
_____

Am I holding any grudges toward my mate?

_____
_____
_____
_____
_____
_____
_____
_____
_____
_____
_____
_____
_____
_____

MAY 16

MAY 17

My wish for my spouse is that…

_____
_____
_____
_____
_____
_____
_____
_____
_____
_____
_____
_____
_____
_____
_____
_____
_____

What am I wanting from my marriage?
What do I bring to my marriage?

_____
_____
_____
_____
_____
_____
_____
_____
_____
_____
_____
_____
_____

MAY 18

MAY 19

Am I sexually satisfied in our marriage?

_____
_____
_____
_____
_____
_____
_____
_____
_____
_____
_____
_____
_____
_____

What is the next big thing
we are believing God for?

_____
_____
_____
_____
_____
_____
_____
_____
_____
_____
_____
_____

MAY 20

MAY 21

Do we view one another as teammates or does our actions show we may be operating as though we are against one another?

_____
_____
_____
_____
_____
_____
_____
_____
_____
_____
_____
_____
_____
_____
_____
_____
_____

In what way do I hide feelings and opinions from my mate? Do I tell them when I'm hurting, what I do not like about situations, or this is what I need?

_____
_____
_____
_____
_____
_____
_____
_____
_____
_____
_____
_____
_____
_____

MAY 22

MAY 23

Am I doing what I truly want to be doing in life and how is being or not being about my purpose affecting my life and marriage?

_____
_____
_____
_____
_____
_____
_____
_____
_____
_____
_____
_____
_____
_____

My marriage needs prayer in what areas?

_____
_____
_____
_____
_____
_____
_____
_____
_____
_____
_____

MAY 24

MAY 25

What makes me want to love my spouse for the rest of our lives?

_____
_____
_____
_____
_____
_____
_____
_____
_____
_____
_____
_____
_____
_____
_____
_____

My spouse reminds me of
God's love the most, when...

_____
_____
_____
_____
_____
_____
_____
_____
_____
_____
_____
_____

MAY 26

MAY 27

I am proud of our union because...

_____
_____
_____
_____
_____
_____
_____
_____
_____
_____
_____
_____
_____
_____

In a mature marriage, we make the decision to act like adults instead of children. Do I handle situations like an adult? Is there any areas I need to grow up?

_____
_____
_____
_____
_____
_____
_____
_____
_____
_____
_____
_____
_____

MAY 28

MAY 29

We went to school to learn and we were trained for our jobs. Did you properly prepare for marriage? If not, what could I have done to be better prepared?

_____
_____
_____
_____
_____
_____
_____
_____
_____
_____
_____
_____
_____

Is our marriage experiencing any fragile moments or situations that we need to be extremely sensitive to? What are ways we can promote healing?

_____
_____
_____
_____
_____
_____
_____
_____
_____
_____
_____
_____

MAY 30

MAY 31

Do we have what it takes to make it through the hard times?

_____

_____

_____

_____

_____

_____

_____

_____

_____

_____

_____

_____

_____

_____

_____

_____

_____

_____

_____

_____

_____

_____

_____

_____

June 1

What am I praying that
God changes in my spouse?

_____
_____
_____
_____
_____
_____
_____
_____
_____
_____
_____
_____
_____
_____

If God never changes my spouse, how can I
change the ways I interact with my spouse?

_____
_____
_____
_____
_____
_____
_____
_____
_____
_____
_____
_____

June 2

June 3

What went really well with my marriage today?

_____
_____
_____
_____
_____
_____
_____
_____
_____
_____
_____
_____
_____

I am hoping this journal helps us to...
or
if we have been using Pillow Talk for a while, what
has it helped us to accomplish...

_____
_____
_____
_____
_____
_____
_____
_____
_____
_____
_____

June 4

June 5

A wish for my marriage is...

_____
_____
_____
_____
_____
_____
_____
_____
_____
_____
_____
_____
_____
_____

What are my spouse's
weaknesses and how do I handle them?

_____
_____
_____
_____
_____
_____
_____
_____
_____
_____
_____
_____
_____

June 6

Do we allow emotions to build up or are we able to discuss things quickly and keep accounts small? How does this affect our marriage?

June 7

_____
_____
_____
_____
_____
_____
_____
_____
_____
_____
_____
_____
_____

Are we focused on the little things that matter such as friendship and dating, talking and touching, being polite and appreciating one another?

June 8

_____
_____
_____
_____
_____
_____
_____
_____
_____
_____
_____

June 9

How does the difference of opinions or the way we handle things, between my spouse and I, make me feel and affect our marriage?

_____
_____
_____
_____
_____
_____
_____
_____
_____
_____
_____
_____
_____
_____
_____
_____

It would be totally euphoric for me if we did...

_____
_____
_____
_____
_____
_____
_____
_____
_____
_____
_____
_____
_____

June 10

June 11

Is there a sense of oneness in our marriage?

_____
_____
_____
_____
_____
_____
_____
_____
_____
_____
_____
_____
_____

What do I need to thank God for?

_____
_____
_____
_____
_____
_____
_____
_____
_____
_____
_____
_____

June 12

June 13

What are some positive things I need to add to my life? What are some negative things I need to remove from my life and marriage?

_____
_____
_____
_____
_____
_____
_____
_____
_____
_____
_____
_____
_____
_____
_____

What ideas (new or old) would I like to incorporate in our relationship to achieve an extraordinary marriage?

_____
_____
_____
_____
_____
_____
_____
_____
_____
_____
_____
_____
_____
_____

June 14

June 15

When my spouse is communicating feelings,
do I really listen to my spouse to seek understanding
or to compose an attack?

_____
_____
_____
_____
_____
_____
_____
_____
_____
_____
_____
_____
_____
_____

Do I allow or create negative things in my life that
has the potential to damage my marriage or am I
diligent in guarding my marriage?

_____
_____
_____
_____
_____
_____
_____
_____
_____
_____
_____
_____
_____

June 16

June 17

What needs our attention and focus at this present time to keep our marriage strong?

_____
_____
_____
_____
_____
_____
_____
_____
_____
_____
_____
_____
_____

Today, I need to thank my spouse for...

_____
_____
_____
_____
_____
_____
_____
_____
_____
_____
_____
_____

June 18

June 19

I love that my mate does…

_____
_____
_____
_____
_____
_____
_____
_____
_____
_____
_____
_____
_____
_____

Our next free weekend, we should…

_____
_____
_____
_____
_____
_____
_____
_____
_____
_____
_____
_____

June 20

June 21

Is there a sense of peace within our marriage?
Does it reflect the type of marriage Christ would
want us to have?

_____
_____
_____
_____
_____
_____
_____
_____
_____
_____
_____
_____
_____
_____

What are some ways we have grown this year?

_____
_____
_____
_____
_____
_____
_____
_____
_____
_____
_____
_____
_____
_____

June 22

June 23

What is our biggest marital challenge right now?

_____
_____
_____
_____
_____
_____
_____
_____
_____
_____
_____
_____
_____

Am I kind to my spouse or do I treat
outsiders better than my spouse?

_____
_____
_____
_____
_____
_____
_____
_____
_____
_____
_____
_____

June 24

June 25

In what areas could I be
more patient with my spouse?

_____
_____
_____
_____
_____
_____
_____
_____
_____
_____
_____
_____
_____
_____

How do I feel about renewing our vows?
If we take that step when and how would we like
the renewal to be done?

_____
_____
_____
_____
_____
_____
_____
_____
_____
_____
_____
_____
_____

June 26

Describe your mate...

_____
_____
_____
_____
_____
_____
_____
_____
_____
_____
_____
_____
_____
_____

Is there something new you would like to try to add in the bedroom to spice up our love life?

_____
_____
_____
_____
_____
_____
_____
_____
_____
_____
_____
_____
_____

June 29

Write some encouraging words to your spouse about a goal they are working on.

_____

_____

_____

_____

_____

_____

_____

_____

_____

_____

_____

_____

_____

What are we trusting God for?

_____

_____

_____

_____

_____

_____

_____

_____

_____

_____

_____

June 30

I am extremely grateful for my spouse because...

_____

_____

_____

_____

_____

—— JULY 1 ——

_____

_____

_____

_____

_____

_____

_____

_____

How do I feel about my mate?
Are my inner thoughts toward my mate
hurtful or healing?

_____

_____

_____

_____

_____

—— JULY 2 ——

_____

_____

_____

_____

_____

What sexual activities do I enjoy the most?
Which ones are uncomfortable for me?

—— JULY 3 ——

_____

_____

_____

_____

_____

_____

_____

_____

_____

_____

_____

_____

We really should....

_____

_____

_____

_____

_____

_____

_____

_____

_____

—— JULY 4 ——

Have we discovered any secrets
to a life-long marriage?

_____

_____

_____

_____

_____

_____

_____

_____

_____

_____

_____

_____

—— JULY 5 ——

What am I looking forward to this month?

_____

_____

_____

_____

_____

_____

_____

_____

_____

_____

_____

—— JULY 6 ——

My favorite activity we do together is...

_____
_____
_____
_____
_____

—— JULY 7 ——

_____
_____
_____
_____
_____
_____
_____

It makes me feel like I am a great spouse when I...

_____
_____
_____
_____

—— JULY 8 ——

_____
_____
_____
_____
_____

What are some new hobbies
we can indulge in together?

———— JULY 9 ————

_____
_____
_____
_____
_____
_____
_____
_____
_____
_____
_____
_____
_____

What Is the most beautiful thing
about your marriage?

_____
_____
_____
_____
_____
_____
_____
_____
_____
_____

———— JULY 10 ————

What did our parent's examples of
relationships teach us about marriage?
Are these examples we want to follow?

—— JULY 11 ——

_____

_____

_____

_____

_____

_____

_____

_____

_____

_____

_____

_____

_____

Do you feel wanted and needed by your spouse?
What makes you feel that way?

—— JULY 12 ——

_____

_____

_____

_____

_____

_____

_____

_____

_____

_____

If we had a chance to take a trip,
where would you want to go?

——— JULY 13 ———

_____
_____
_____
_____
_____
_____
_____
_____
_____
_____
_____
_____

Something that my spouse does
that makes me laugh is...

_____
_____
_____
_____
_____
_____
_____
_____
_____
_____

——— JULY 14 ———

What are your thoughts
towards sex within our marriage?
What purpose does it serve for our marriage?

—— JULY 15 ——

_____
_____
_____
_____
_____
_____
_____
_____
_____
_____
_____
_____
_____

I remember when we...

_____
_____
_____
_____
_____
_____
_____
_____
_____
_____

—— JULY 16 ——

What goal can we work on, together, this week?

_____
_____
_____
_____
_____
_____
_____
_____
_____
_____
_____
_____
_____

———— JULY 17 ————

I love to call my spouse _____,
and I love when they call me _____?

_____
_____
_____
_____
_____
_____
_____
_____
_____
_____
_____

———— JULY 18 ————

How can I use my marriage to inspire others?

———— JULY 19 ————

_____
_____
_____
_____
_____
_____
_____
_____
_____
_____
_____
_____
_____

According to their actions,
I think my spouse's highest priority is...

_____
_____
_____
_____
_____
_____
_____
_____
_____
_____
_____

———— JULY 20 ————

Do I seek to understand my mate's perspective
with empathy for what they are dealing with?

—————— JULY 21 ——————

_____

_____

_____

_____

_____

_____

_____

_____

_____

_____

_____

My spouse is very important to me,
how can I show them that today?

_____

_____

_____

_____

——————— JULY 22———————

_____

_____

_____

_____

_____

_____

_____

What am I personally working
on to make my marriage better?

——— JULY 23 ———

_____
_____
_____
_____
_____
_____
_____
_____
_____
_____
_____
_____

Do I trust my spouse?

_____
_____
_____
_____
_____
_____
_____
_____
_____
_____
_____
_____

——— JULY 24 ———

I rate my marriage, on a scale of 1-10 as...

_____
_____
_____
_____
_____
_____
_____
_____
_____
_____
_____
_____
_____
_____
_____

—JULY 25—

Does my marriage honor God?

_____
_____
_____
_____
_____
_____
_____
_____
_____
_____

—JULY 26—

What advice would I give to a
young couple on their wedding day?

————JULY 27————

_____
_____
_____
_____
_____
_____
_____
_____
_____
_____
_____
_____
_____
_____

Do I believe it's possible to have a marriage in
which everything is handled in a healthy way?
What did/does it take to get to this stage in
marriage?

————JULY 28————

_____
_____
_____
_____
_____
_____
_____
_____
_____
_____
_____

It was really sweet of my spouse to...

_____
_____
_____
_____
_____
_____
_____
_____
_____
_____
_____
_____
_____

—JULY 29—

I am so happy for my spouse because...

_____
_____
_____
_____
_____
_____
_____
_____
_____
_____
_____

—JULY 30—

When my spouse is having a rough day, do I usually respond with aggravation or compassion?

_____
_____
_____
_____
_____
_____
_____
_____
_____
_____

—— JULY 31 ——

_____
_____
_____
_____
_____
_____
_____
_____
_____
_____
_____
_____
_____
_____
_____

Do I feel as if my spouse
has my best interest at heart?

AUGUST 1

_____
_____
_____
_____
_____
_____
_____
_____
_____
_____
_____

How can I help my spouse today?

_____
_____
_____
_____
_____
_____
_____
_____
_____
_____

AUGUST 2

What mini-rituals do we have
together, that we look forward to?

AUGUST 3

_____
_____
_____
_____
_____
_____
_____
_____
_____
_____
_____
_____

What's something positive that I saw my mate
doing recently that I failed to acknowledge it and
should do it now?

_____
_____
_____
_____
_____
_____
_____
_____
_____
_____
_____

AUGUST 4

What things do I intentionally do to
make my spouse feel loved?

AUGUST 5

_____
_____
_____
_____
_____
_____
_____
_____
_____
_____
_____
_____

What grudges are we holding that
we need to acknowledge or let go?

_____
_____
_____
_____
_____
_____
_____
_____
_____
_____

AUGUST 6

In what ways do I attempt to change my spouse
instead of accepting them for who they are?

AUGUST 7

_____
_____
_____
_____
_____
_____
_____
_____
_____
_____
_____
_____
_____

What would be an ideal way for
my spouse and I to address difficult feelings?

_____
_____
_____
_____
_____
_____
_____
_____
_____
_____
_____
_____

AUGUST 8

Am I consistently intentional about my marriage
or do I just allow things to happen?

AUGUST 9

_____
_____
_____
_____
_____
_____
_____
_____
_____
_____
_____
_____
_____

When was the last time I encouraged and built up
my spouse with positive words and actions?

_____
_____
_____
_____
_____
_____
_____
_____
_____
_____
_____

AUGUST 10

Is there stress in our lives that
we need to be conscious of?

AUGUST 11

_____
_____
_____
_____
_____
_____
_____
_____
_____
_____
_____
_____

Make a checklist of some things
I want us to accomplish together.

_____
_____
_____
_____
_____
_____
_____
_____
_____
_____
_____

AUGUST 12

What do I remember most from our wedding day?

_____
_____
_____
_____
_____
_____
_____
_____
_____
_____
_____
_____

AUGUST 13

When I think of my mate and a song,
what is the first song that comes to mind?

_____
_____
_____
_____
_____
_____
_____
_____
_____
_____
_____

AUGUST 14

How important is it to us to
keep regular "date nights"?

_____
_____
_____
_____
_____
_____
_____
_____
_____
_____
_____
_____

AUGUST 15

Do I feel connected to my spouse?

_____
_____
_____
_____
_____
_____
_____
_____
_____
_____

AUGUST 16

Have we learned to handle conflict effectively?

_____
_____
_____
_____
_____
_____
_____
_____
_____
_____
_____
_____

AUGUST 17

What is the first or next marriage book we should
read to gain more understanding about marriage?

_____
_____
_____
_____
_____
_____
_____
_____
_____
_____

AUGUST 18

What can I give to my spouse to help them overcome what they are dealing with at the present moment?

AUGUST 19

_____
_____
_____
_____
_____
_____
_____
_____
_____
_____
_____
_____
_____
_____

Who are other married couples we hang around and are they good examples for our marriage?

_____
_____
_____
_____
_____
_____
_____
_____
_____
_____
_____

AUGUST 20

Am I mature enough to love my spouse
even when they are behaving unlovingly?

AUGUST 21

_____
_____
_____
_____
_____
_____
_____
_____
_____
_____
_____

Where do we stand financially?
Do we argue about money or have an
understanding?

_____
_____
_____
_____
_____
_____
_____
_____
_____
_____

AUGUST 22

AUGUST 23

_____
_____
_____
_____
_____
_____
_____
_____
_____
_____
_____
_____
_____

Do we have an understanding that a groom needs
unconditional respect and a bride needs
unconditional love?

_____
_____
_____
_____
_____
_____
_____
_____
_____
_____
_____
_____

AUGUST 24

What chore can I do for my spouse this week that would really help them out?

_____
_____
_____
_____
_____
_____
_____
_____
_____
_____
_____
_____
_____

AUGUST 25

What is my Love Language,
according to Dr. Gary Chapman?
What is my spouses Love Language?

_____
_____
_____
_____
_____
_____
_____
_____
_____
_____
_____

AUGUST 26

Are there any issues threatening our marriage that we need to seek help and advice from our mentor or counselor?

AUGUST 27

_____
_____
_____
_____
_____
_____
_____
_____
_____
_____
_____
_____
_____

What is something I want my spouse to know and understand about me?

_____
_____
_____
_____
_____
_____
_____
_____
_____
_____
_____

AUGUST 28

What does my spouse need from me?

_____
_____
_____
_____
_____
_____
_____
_____
_____
_____
_____
_____
_____

AUGUST 29

How can I help make my spouse more successful?

_____
_____
_____
_____
_____
_____
_____
_____
_____
_____
_____
_____

AUGUST 30

AUGUST 31

Do we keep our private matters to ourselves and our mentors or do we outwardly express our problems in ways that could be harmful to our marriage?

_____
_____
_____
_____
_____
_____
_____
_____
_____
_____
_____
_____
_____

_____
_____
_____
_____
_____
_____
_____
_____
_____
_____
_____
_____
_____
_____

Have my spouse and I committed
"until death do us part?"

SEPTEMBER 1

_____
_____
_____
_____
_____
_____
_____
_____
_____
_____
_____
_____

Do we enjoy have enough dates
and quality time together?

_____
_____
_____
_____
_____
_____
_____
_____
_____
_____
_____

SEPTEMBER 2

In what area does my mate
challenge me the most?

SEPTEMBER 3

_____
_____
_____
_____
_____
_____
_____
_____
_____
_____
_____
_____
_____

Do we go to bed angry or do
we diffuse arguments before bedtime?

_____
_____
_____
_____
_____
_____
_____
_____
_____
_____
_____
_____

SEPTEMBER 4

What is something we have not experienced together that we definitely should make plans for?

SEPTEMBER 5

_____
_____
_____
_____
_____
_____
_____
_____
_____
_____
_____
_____
_____

My spouse is beautiful because...

_____
_____
_____
_____
_____
_____
_____
_____
_____
_____

SEPTEMBER 6

How does the attitude I carry about life,
personally affect our marriage?

SEPTEMBER 7

_____
_____
_____
_____
_____
_____
_____
_____
_____
_____
_____
_____
_____
_____
_____

Use this space to compliment your spouse...

_____
_____
_____
_____
_____
_____
_____
_____
_____
_____
_____

SEPTEMBER 8

What was my first impression of my mate?

SEPTEMBER 9

_____
_____
_____
_____
_____
_____
_____
_____
_____
_____
_____
_____
_____
_____

How has my mate brought
laughter and smiles into my life recently?

_____
_____
_____
_____
_____
_____
_____
_____
_____
_____
_____
_____

SEPTEMBER 10

What habits am I aware that I possess that bothers my spouse the most? Am I willing to work on those habits?

SEPTEMBER 11

_____
_____
_____
_____
_____
_____
_____
_____
_____
_____
_____
_____
_____
_____
_____

What do I complain about most when it comes to marriage? What is a better way I can approach my spouse about the situations?

_____
_____
_____
_____
_____
_____
_____
_____
_____
_____
_____

SEPTEMBER 12

Am I enjoying this season of my marriage?

_____

SEPTEMBER 13

_____
_____
_____
_____
_____
_____
_____
_____
_____
_____
_____
_____
_____
_____
_____
_____

What do we need to move
to the top of our priority list?

_____
_____
_____
_____
_____
_____
_____
_____
_____
_____
_____

SEPTEMBER 14

If money was no problem,
how would our dream house look?

SEPTEMBER 15

_____
_____
_____
_____
_____
_____
_____
_____
_____
_____
_____
_____
_____
_____

In what area does my spouse need my support?

_____
_____
_____
_____
_____
_____
_____
_____
_____
_____

SEPTEMBER 16

Does my spouse's actions in marriage make it easy or hard for me to trust that they will protect me in all situations?

_____
_____
_____
_____
_____
_____
_____
_____
_____
_____
_____
_____
_____

SEPTEMBER 17

Do we do our fair share of chores in our relationship?

_____
_____
_____
_____
_____
_____
_____
_____
_____
_____
_____

SEPTEMBER 18

If we were a "Powerful Influential" Couple,
what would we want to be known for?

SEPTEMBER 19

_____
_____
_____
_____
_____
_____
_____
_____
_____
_____
_____
_____

What things do we do that creates an
atmosphere of laughter and fun in our marriage?

_____
_____
_____
_____
_____
_____
_____
_____
_____
_____
_____

SEPTEMBER 20

What bad habits do we have that affects our marriage negatively?

SEPTEMBER 21

_____
_____
_____
_____
_____
_____
_____
_____
_____
_____
_____
_____
_____
_____
_____

Am I giving my spouse my best?

_____
_____
_____
_____
_____
_____
_____
_____
_____
_____
_____
_____
_____

SEPTEMBER 22

What has helped us stay together and not give up on us?

SEPTEMBER 23

_____
_____
_____
_____
_____
_____
_____
_____
_____
_____
_____
_____
_____
_____

How vulnerable do I allow
myself to be with my spouse?

_____
_____
_____
_____
_____
_____
_____
_____
_____
_____
_____
_____

SEPTEMBER 24

What have I been trying to tell my spouse that I wish they would hear and understand?

SEPTEMBER 25

_____
_____
_____
_____
_____
_____
_____
_____
_____
_____
_____
_____
_____
_____

I refuse to give up on my spouse because…

_____
_____
_____
_____
_____
_____
_____
_____
_____
_____
_____
_____

SEPTEMBER 26

Do I focus more on my marriage than my career?

_____

_____

_____

_____

_____

_____

_____

_____

_____

_____

_____

_____

_____

SEPTEMBER 27

Do we have a healthy marriage?

_____

_____

_____

_____

_____

_____

_____

_____

_____

_____

_____

SEPTEMBER 28

Is there anything present in my life that I need to set boundaries to make sure my marriage is protected?

SEPTEMBER 29

_____
_____
_____
_____
_____
_____
_____
_____
_____
_____
_____
_____
_____

I'm noticing my mate has been "crying out" for...

_____
_____
_____
_____
_____
_____
_____
_____
_____
_____
_____

SEPTEMBER 30

I love when my mate...

_____
_____
_____
_____
_____
_____
_____
_____
_____
_____
_____
_____
_____
_____

OCTOBER 1

Our sex life is...

_____
_____
_____
_____
_____
_____
_____
_____
_____
_____
_____

OCTOBER 2

The best thing my mate has given me is…

_____
_____
_____
_____
_____
_____
_____
_____
_____
_____
_____
_____
_____
_____

OCTOBER 3

I really loved when…

_____
_____
_____
_____
_____
_____
_____
_____
_____
_____
_____
_____

OCTOBER 4

I'm incredibly grateful for...

_____

_____

_____

_____

_____

_____

_____

_____

_____

_____

_____

_____

_____

OCTOBER 5

I am needing...

_____

_____

_____

_____

_____

_____

_____

_____

_____

_____

OCTOBER 6

What and/or how much do I know about my spouse's future dreams?

_____
_____
_____
_____
_____
_____
_____
_____
_____
_____
_____
_____
_____
_____

OCTOBER 7

Describe how you felt and what you remember about the first kiss you shared…

_____
_____
_____
_____
_____
_____
_____
_____
_____
_____
_____
_____

OCTOBER 8

When did you find yourself
becoming attracted to your spouse?

OCTOBER 9

_____
_____
_____
_____
_____
_____
_____
_____
_____
_____
_____

Marriage has taught me...

_____
_____
_____
_____
_____
_____
_____
_____
_____
_____

OCTOBER 10

What do you like most about your mate?

_____
_____
_____
_____
_____
_____
_____
_____
_____
_____
_____
_____

OCTOBER 11

Instead of expecting my spouse to read my mind,
I should simply express...

_____
_____
_____
_____
_____
_____
_____
_____
_____

OCTOBER 12

The best thing about being married is…

_____
_____
_____
_____
_____
_____
_____
_____
_____
_____
_____
_____
_____
_____

OCTOBER 13

Do I take care of myself sufficiently
to have enough energy to give to my marriage?

_____
_____
_____
_____
_____
_____
_____
_____
_____
_____
_____

OCTOBER 14

What are my beliefs and thoughts about my marriage and my spouse?

OCTOBER 15

_____
_____
_____
_____
_____
_____
_____
_____
_____
_____
_____
_____
_____
_____
_____

Is our home a place of peace for us?

_____
_____
_____
_____
_____
_____
_____
_____
_____
_____
_____

OCTOBER 16

Why did I get married?

_____

_____

_____

_____

_____

_____

_____

_____

_____

_____

_____

_____

_____

OCTOBER 17

What do we still want to accomplish
before the end of the year?

_____

_____

_____

_____

_____

_____

_____

_____

_____

_____

_____

_____

OCTOBER 18

What's one of my favorite stories
we've created as a couple...

_____
_____
_____
_____
_____
_____
_____
_____
_____
_____
_____
_____
_____
_____

OCTOBER 19

Tell your spouse what you need from them...

_____
_____
_____
_____
_____
_____
_____
_____
_____
_____
_____
_____

OCTOBER 20

How is our friendship with one another?

_____
_____
_____
_____
_____
_____
_____
_____
_____
_____
_____
_____
_____

OCTOBER 21

Write a simple note to your spouse letting them
know how much you love them...

_____
_____
_____
_____
_____
_____
_____
_____
_____
_____
_____

OCTOBER 22

Is there anything that makes me feel
insecure in our marriage?

OCTOBER 23

_____
_____
_____
_____
_____
_____
_____
_____
_____
_____
_____
_____
_____
_____
_____

What are some way I see myself blessing and
serving my spouse for the remainder of the month?

_____
_____
_____
_____
_____
_____
_____
_____
_____
_____
_____

OCTOBER 24

List the places we've traveled together.

_____
_____
_____
_____
_____
_____
_____
_____
_____
_____
_____
_____
_____

OCTOBER 25

Do we get enough "personal space and time?"

_____
_____
_____
_____
_____
_____
_____
_____
_____
_____
_____
_____

OCTOBER 26

I need my mate to forgive me for...

_____
_____
_____
_____
_____
_____
_____
_____
_____
_____
_____
_____

OCTOBER 27

Do I speak my spouse's love language or do I try to
love them in the way I want to be loved?

_____
_____
_____
_____
_____
_____
_____
_____
_____
_____
_____

OCTOBER 28

Does our marriage make our lives better?

_____

_____

_____

_____

_____

_____

_____

_____

_____

_____

_____

_____

_____

OCTOBER 29

Write and tell your spouse why you "like" them.

_____

_____

_____

_____

_____

_____

_____

_____

_____

_____

_____

_____

_____

OCTOBER 30

Do I feel there is a level of intimacy and passion in our marriage? Do I feel a connection to my mate in this present moment? Why?

OCTOBER 31

_____

_____

_____

_____

_____

_____

_____

_____

_____

_____

_____

_____

_____

_____

_____

_____

_____

_____

_____

_____

_____

_____

_____

_____

_____

_____

_____

_____

NOVEMBER 1

What am I most grateful for in my life?

_____
_____
_____
_____
_____
_____
_____
_____
_____
_____
_____
_____
_____
_____

NOVEMBER 2

Who do we know that could use some help from us? How can we reach out to help?

_____
_____
_____
_____
_____
_____
_____
_____
_____
_____
_____

NOVEMBER
3

I really thank God for...

_____
_____
_____
_____
_____
_____
_____
_____
_____
_____
_____
_____
_____
_____

I am so happy and grateful now that...

_____
_____
_____
_____
_____
_____
_____
_____
_____
_____
_____
_____
_____

NOVEMBER
4

I am grateful for my spouse's friendship because...

NOVEMBER
5

_____
_____
_____
_____
_____
_____
_____
_____
_____
_____
_____
_____

I am thankful for my spouse's health because...

_____
_____
_____
_____
_____
_____
_____
_____
_____
_____
_____

NOVEMBER
6

NOVEMBER
7

I am grateful for our jobs because...

_____
_____
_____
_____
_____
_____
_____
_____
_____
_____
_____
_____
_____

I am grateful for our hard times because...

_____
_____
_____
_____
_____
_____
_____
_____
_____
_____
_____

NOVEMBER
8

I am grateful for our family because…

NOVEMBER
9

_____
_____
_____
_____
_____
_____
_____
_____
_____
_____
_____
_____
_____
_____

I am grateful for our home because…

_____
_____
_____
_____
_____
_____
_____
_____
_____
_____
_____
_____
_____

NOVEMBER
10

NOVEMBER
11

I am thankful for my spouse because...

_____
_____
_____
_____
_____
_____
_____
_____
_____
_____
_____
_____
_____
_____

I am thankful we have overcame...

_____
_____
_____
_____
_____
_____
_____
_____
_____
_____
_____
_____

NOVEMBER
12

NOVEMBER 13

I am thankful for my spouse's touch because…

_____
_____
_____
_____
_____
_____
_____
_____
_____
_____
_____
_____
_____
_____

My spouse has made a difference in my life because…

_____
_____
_____
_____
_____
_____
_____
_____
_____
_____
_____
_____

NOVEMBER 14

NOVEMBER
15

I thank God for...

_____
_____
_____
_____
_____
_____
_____
_____
_____
_____
_____
_____
_____
_____

I am a fortunate person because...

_____
_____
_____
_____
_____
_____
_____
_____
_____
_____
_____
_____
_____

NOVEMBER
16

NOVEMBER

17

We are thankful for the opportunity to...

_____
_____
_____
_____
_____
_____
_____
_____
_____
_____
_____
_____
_____

What marital experiences are you most thankful for?

_____
_____
_____
_____
_____
_____
_____
_____
_____
_____
_____

NOVEMBER

18

NOVEMBER
19

_____
_____
_____
_____
_____
_____
_____
_____
_____
_____
_____
_____
_____
_____

My spouse helps me so much with…

_____
_____
_____
_____
_____
_____
_____
_____
_____
_____
_____

NOVEMBER
20

I am thankful my spouse and I are in a position to...

NOVEMBER
21

_____
_____
_____
_____
_____
_____
_____
_____
_____
_____
_____
_____
_____

I am grateful I am able to benefit my spouse by...

_____
_____
_____
_____
_____
_____
_____
_____
_____
_____
_____
_____

NOVEMBER
22

NOVEMBER

23

_____
_____
_____
_____
_____
_____
_____
_____
_____
_____
_____

What is different from one year ago that we have
to be thankful for?

_____
_____
_____
_____
_____
_____
_____
_____
_____
_____

NOVEMBER

24

If we could thank 5 people who have helped our marriage, who would they be...

NOVEMBER

25

_____
_____
_____
_____
_____
_____
_____
_____
_____
_____
_____
_____
_____
_____

I thank my spouse for understanding me when...

_____
_____
_____
_____
_____
_____
_____
_____
_____
_____
_____
_____
_____

NOVEMBER

26

What needs could you thank your spouse for meeting?

NOVEMBER
27

_____
_____
_____
_____
_____
_____
_____
_____
_____
_____
_____
_____
_____
_____

What bitter trials have we endured that turned out to be "blessings in disguised?"

_____
_____
_____
_____
_____
_____
_____
_____
_____
_____
_____
_____
_____
_____

NOVEMBER
28

NOVEMBER
29

List 10 miracles you have to be thankful for…

_____
_____
_____
_____
_____
_____
_____
_____
_____
_____
_____
_____
_____
_____

God has kept His promises and been faithful in our lives and marriage. Write a letter of thanksgiving to God

_____
_____
_____
_____
_____
_____
_____
_____
_____
_____
_____
_____

NOVEMBER
30

All I want for Christmas is...

December

1

_____
_____
_____
_____
_____
_____
_____
_____
_____
_____
_____
_____
_____
_____

What is your favorite bible verse?

_____
_____
_____
_____
_____
_____
_____
_____
_____
_____
_____
_____

December

2

One way we plan to finish this
year strong as a couple is...

December

3

_____
_____
_____
_____
_____
_____
_____
_____
_____
_____
_____
_____
_____

When you look at your spouse,
what is the first thing you notice?

_____
_____
_____
_____
_____
_____
_____
_____
_____
_____
_____

December

4

Something my mate does right in our marriage is...

_____
_____
_____
_____
_____
_____
_____
_____
_____
_____
_____
_____

December

5

I feel most appreciated in our marriage when...

_____
_____
_____
_____
_____
_____
_____
_____
_____
_____

December

6

December

7

_____
_____
_____
_____
_____
_____
_____
_____
_____
_____
_____
_____
_____
_____

Do I feel like my spouse is being a good spouse to me? Am I being good to my spouse?

_____
_____
_____
_____
_____
_____
_____
_____
_____
_____
_____

December

8

One bucket list adventure I want
to experience with my mate is...

December

9

_____
_____
_____
_____
_____
_____
_____
_____
_____
_____
_____
_____
_____

Write out some advice to yourself about how
to get to the next level in your marriage.

_____
_____
_____
_____
_____
_____
_____
_____
_____
_____
_____

December

10

When I "picture us together", it makes me feel...

_____
_____
_____
_____
_____
_____
_____
_____
_____
_____
_____
_____
_____
_____
_____
_____

December

11

What 3 skills should I acquire to
make sure my marriage last for a lifetime?

_____
_____
_____
_____
_____
_____
_____
_____
_____
_____
_____

December

12

How did I know my spouse was "the one?"

_____
_____
_____
_____
_____
_____
_____
_____
_____
_____
_____
_____
_____

December
13

The best gift my spouse has given me was...

_____
_____
_____
_____
_____
_____
_____
_____
_____
_____

December
14

If my spouse could only give me 3 things for the rest of our lives, I would ask for...

_____
_____
_____
_____
_____
_____
_____
_____
_____
_____
_____
_____
_____

December

15

What is the best thing that has happened in our marriage?

_____
_____
_____
_____
_____
_____
_____
_____
_____
_____
_____

December

16

December

17

_____

_____

_____

_____

_____

_____

_____

_____

_____

_____

_____

_____

_____

_____

One thing I should give of myself,
to my mate, right now, is...

_____

_____

_____

_____

_____

_____

_____

_____

_____

_____

_____

December

18

It is really fun when we...

_____
_____
_____
_____
_____
_____
_____
_____
_____
_____
_____
_____
_____
_____

December
19

What is our biggest accomplishment,
thus far, as a couple?

_____
_____
_____
_____
_____
_____
_____
_____
_____
_____
_____
_____
_____

December
20

_____
_____
_____
_____
_____
_____
_____
_____
_____
_____
_____
_____
_____

December
21

Does our marriage reflect peace and joy?

_____
_____
_____
_____
_____
_____
_____
_____
_____
_____
_____

December
22

My favorite Christmas memory
I have of us would be?

December
23

_____
_____
_____
_____
_____
_____
_____
_____
_____
_____
_____
_____
_____
_____

I wish...

_____
_____
_____
_____
_____
_____
_____
_____
_____
_____
_____

December
24

Spending Christmas with you is...

_____
_____
_____
_____
_____
_____
_____
_____
_____
_____
_____
_____
_____
_____

December

25

To start living more fully,
passionate, and alive, we should...

_____
_____
_____
_____
_____
_____
_____
_____
_____
_____
_____
_____
_____

December

26

December
27

_____
_____
_____
_____
_____
_____
_____
_____
_____
_____
_____
_____
_____
_____
_____
_____

What is our dream vacation for next year?

_____
_____
_____
_____
_____
_____
_____
_____
_____
_____
_____
_____

December
28

What are 10 things you will
achieve together in the next year?

December

29

_____
_____
_____
_____
_____
_____
_____
_____
_____
_____
_____
_____
_____
_____

What was your favorite moment of this year?

_____
_____
_____
_____
_____
_____
_____
_____
_____
_____
_____
_____
_____

December

30

December
31

_____
_____
_____
_____
_____
_____
_____
_____
_____
_____

_____
_____
_____
_____
_____
_____
_____
_____
_____
_____
_____
_____
_____
_____